Stocking Stuffers: I Spy Christmas Book For Kids Ages 2-5:

A Fun Activity Book with Guessing Games for Toddlers, Preschool & Kindergarten to Learn Phonics & Reading Skills | Christmas Gifts for Kids

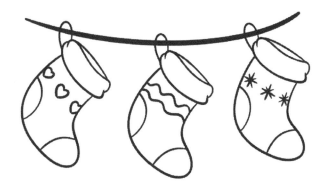

ISBN: 979-8864223574

This Book Belongs to:

_____

_____

Christmas is a time when we celebrate the birthday of Jesus.
It's a season of joy and lots of shared family moments, marked by tree decorating and exchanging gifts, symbolizing love, peace, and goodwill.

So, who is ready for a Christmas journey with this book?

HOW TO PLAY:
See the pictures and find the item that starts with the given letter.
Look on the next page for the answer, and try to pronounce it correctly.
Have Fun and Color the pictures!

I SPY with my little eye something beginning with...

ANGEL

I SPY with my little eye something beginning with...

B

BELLS

I SPY with my little eye something beginning with...

CANDLES

I SPY with my little eye something beginning with...

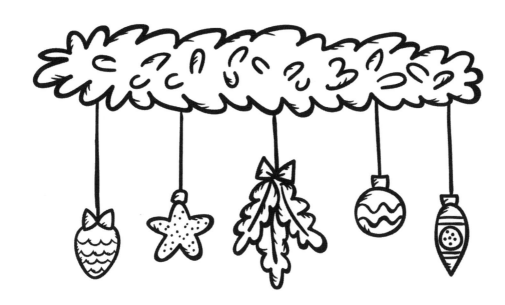

DECORATION

I SPY with my little eye something beginning with...

ELF

FENCE

I SPY with my little eye something beginning with...

G

GIFTS

I SPY with my little eye something beginning with...

HOUSE

I SPY with my little eye something beginning with...

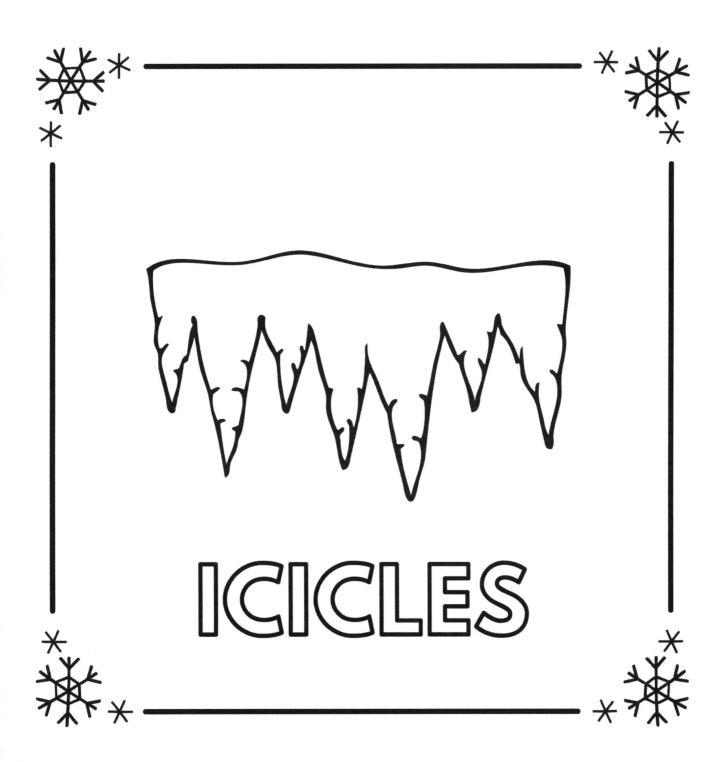

ICICLES

I SPY with my little eye
something beginning with...

JACKET

I SPY with my little eye something beginning with...

KETTLE

I SPY with my little eye something beginning with...

LETTER

I SPY with my little eye something beginning with...

MISTLETOE

I SPY with my little eye something beginning with...

NUTCRACKER

I SPY with my little eye something beginning with...

OWL

I SPY with my little eye something beginning with...

PENGUIN

I SPY with my little eye something beginning with...

QUEEN

I SPY with my little eye
something beginning with...

REINDEER

I SPY with my little eye something beginning with...

SANTA CLAUS

I SPY with my little eye something beginning with...

TEDDY BEAR

I SPY with my little eye something beginning with...

UMBRELLA

I SPY with my little eye something beginning with...

VIXEN

I SPY with my little eye something beginning with...

WREATH

I SPY with my little eye something beginning with...

XMAS TREE

I SPY with my little eye
something beginning with...

YULE LOG

I SPY with my little eye
something beginning with...

ZEBRA

Made in United States
Troutdale, OR
12/04/2023